The people of Etheria love their Princess Adora, who is gentle and good. But there are times when the country is in danger and they need someone of strength to lead them. Those are the times when Princess Adora takes sword in hand to become She-ra, Princess of Power. She rides Swift Wind, her magical winged unicorn, and defends her country and her people against the forces of evil.

British Library Cataloguing in Publication Data

Grant, John, *1930-*
She-ra and the dark pool.—(She-ra princess of power)
I. Title II. Davies, Robin III. Series
823'.914[J] PZ7

ISBN 0-7214-0955-5

First edition

Published by Ladybird Books Ltd Loughborough Leicestershire UK
Ladybird Books Inc Lewiston Maine 04240 USA

Stephanie harris

SHE-RA™

PRINCESS of POWER™

She-ra and the Dark Pool

by John Grant
illustrated by Robin Davies

Ladybird Books

One of the pleasantest places in all Etheria was Whispering Wood. Birds nested in the branches of the tall trees. Deer grazed in sunny glades. Small animals scurried among the grass and flowers. And the Twiggets laughed and played tricks on each other, or on anyone else who happened to be passing.

When Princess Adora rode through the wood on Spirit, her beautiful white horse, all the creatures hurried to greet her. While the princess was amongst them they knew that the Power of Light protected them from evil. They were safe from the wicked mischief of Hordak, and his sinister ally, Shadow Weaver, Mistress of Dark Magic.

There was, however, a part of the wood where even the most adventurous Twigget never ventured. Here was the Dark Pool. It lay in a hollow, surrounded by bare and twisted trees. Instead of grass and flowers, the banks of the pool were covered in slime and poisonous moss. The branches of the trees reached out over the pool in a tangled mass, so thick that the sun never shone through. No birds sang. No breeze rippled the black water.

Streamers of thin mist were the only things that moved in the half light.

The people of Whispering Wood said that the Dark Pool was bottomless.

Some even said that a horrible monster lived in the pool.

But nobody was brave enough to find out for himself.

One evening, Kowl sat perched on a branch. A crowd of young Twiggets played in the grass as the setting sun shone low through the trees. It was a very happy and peaceful scene.

Suddenly it was as if a chill winter breeze had blown through the wood. Kowl ruffled his feathers and shivered. The Twiggets stopped playing and huddled together. A shadow seemed to pass over Whispering Wood.

"What is it?" said the Twiggets.

Kowl peered into the depths of the wood. "Something evil is passing close by," he whispered. "I fear that Shadow Weaver is on the prowl. There is trouble at hand for someone, somewhere."

The shadow passed on. The Twiggets went back to their play in the last of the evening light. They had already forgotten. But Kowl knew that there were evil days to come.

Shadow Weaver stood on the bank of the Dark Pool. Faint moonlight shone through the branches onto the mist swirling about her.

The Mistress of Dark Magic raised her arms and cried:

"BY THE POWERS OF DARKNESS I COMMAND YOU TO RISE AND DO MY BIDDING!"

Beneath the water something moved. The water bubbled and swirled. And a monstrous creature rose to the surface. It stood on the bank, towering over Shadow Weaver. Its eyes glowed red as it looked at her. Then it reached out to seize her.

Shadow Weaver waved her hand, and the monster was bound fast by chains of shadow.

"I have work for you," she cried. "But first, you must learn to obey me!"

"Come," said Shadow Weaver to the creature, "we have far to travel while it is still dark."

By secret paths through the forest, she led the chained monster. A party of woodcutters who had left home before daybreak to work in a distant part of the wood took cover in the bushes at the sound of heavy footsteps and breaking branches. Terrified, they watched the monster pass by almost close enough to touch. Forgetting their work, they hurried

for home to warn their families.

Suddenly, a voice hailed them. It was Bow, the Master Archer. They told him what they had seen. Bow hurried off, and from the branches of a tree saw for himself Shadow Weaver and her creature.

Without wasting a moment, Bow hurried to report to Princess Adora. By daybreak, she and everyone else in Etheria knew of Shadow Weaver's visit to the Dark Pool.

As the moon set, and before the sun had risen, Shadow Weaver and the creature stood at the foot of a high, rocky mountain. At her command two huge doors opened in the side of the mountain. Beyond the doors was a lofty cavern stretching back into black shadow. As Shadow Weaver and the monster passed through the doors, they crashed shut behind them. A moment later the sun rose, bathing the mountain in morning light.

"My Dark Magic has freed you from the cold depths of the Dark Pool!" cried Shadow Weaver. "Do as you are commanded, and you will stay to walk free in the upper world. Disobey, and you will return to the cold darkness for ever!"

The creature bowed its head in obedience.

Shadow Weaver waved her hand, and the chains of shadow vanished.

*   *   *

In his mountain headquarters Hordak listened to Shadow Weaver as she described the monster.

"I have found you a warrior such as you never dreamed of," she said.

"One black giant doesn't make an army!" snarled Hordak.

"This one does," said Shadow Weaver. "Your enemies will soon learn that all their strength and courage are useless against my creature."

"Let *me* be the judge of that!" cried Hordak. "Show me this thing which you have conjured up."

Shadow Weaver took Hordak to the cavern in the mountain. The monster glared down at him with its red eyes. Then, at a signal from Shadow Weaver, it reached out and seized Hordak, lifting him high over its head, and gripping him so that he could hardly breathe. At another signal from the Mistress of Dark Magic, Hordak was set gasping on his feet again.

"I'm convinced," he panted. "From this day, terror will walk the land of Etheria!"

And, just as Hordak had promised, fear and destruction came to Etheria. Soon, everyone had heard of the evil thing which walked the night. As darkness fell, the people barricaded themselves in their homes. Even the wild creatures were not safe. The birds flew to roost in the topmost branches of the tallest trees, and the animals trembled in their dens. By daybreak the monster had gone, leaving a trail of destruction. And at nightfall it appeared again, striding through field and forest, smashing everything in its path.

Some brave Etherians armed themselves and set out to stop the monster. But their weapons proved useless, and they were swept aside as if they were flies.

Princess Adora did what she could to help but as things grew worse, she made up her mind. This was a task for She-ra, Princess of Power. In a secret glade she drew her sword and cried,

"FOR THE HONOUR OF GRAYSKULL!"

Instantly she was She-ra, Princess of Power. In a blaze of magic light from her sword, Spirit became Swift Wind, the fabulous winged unicorn!

Starting from the Dark Pool, She-ra easily followed the trail of destruction left by the monster. The forest trees were smashed to splinters. Buildings lay in ruins. Late in the day, She-ra came to a high, rocky mountain. And here the trail came to an end.

But – there was no monster!

The monster was enormous! It couldn't have simply vanished!

"Up, Swift Wind!" cried She-ra. As she soared close to the side of the mountain she saw the huge doors. "The monster must be inside the mountain," she said to Swift Wind. "Let's take a closer look."

At that moment a harsh voice called out, "So! You have found my pet's hiding place!" It was Hordak, perched above the doors.

"My creature has been enjoying a little gentle exercise so far. Now he is ready to go to work properly. Unless, that is, the people of Etheria obey me as their lord and master. If they do, the doors stay closed. If not...!"

Without wasting a moment more, She-ra put Swift Wind into a fast glide away from the mountain. She had much to do.

As Princess Adora, She-ra hurried to find her faithful friend, Bow. She told him about the door in the mountain. She also told him of Hordak's threat to turn the monster loose again if the people of Etheria did not obey him.

"This will be difficult," said Bow. "Even without the monster, Hordak has a large army of warriors at his command. And the door does not sound like one that can be broken in with a battering ram."

“Why not let Hordak open the door for us?” said Adora. “If the people of Etheria do not obey him, he will open the door to turn the monster loose again.”

“Yes,” said Bow, “and then, we will be waiting!”

Bow set off to get the fighting men of Etheria together. Adora rode into the forest. When she found Kowl, she told him to speak to all the small people of the woods, the animals, birds and, of course, the Twiggets. “They are to keep watch on the door in the mountain,” she said, “and send word the moment it opens again.”

For several days nothing happened. The monster stayed locked inside the mountain.

Then one evening as dusk was falling, a squirrel in the branches of a tree growing close to the mountain heard a loud rumbling. The great doors were swinging open.

The squirrel raced, chattering loudly, through the tree-tops. A black crow heard the squirrel and flapped off into the growing darkness, croaking as it went. A young Twigget heard the crow, and ran as fast as his legs would carry him. He fell in a breathless heap in front of Kowl.

"The oars are dopening!...the ropes are oarning!...the oders are..."

Kowl didn't wait to hear more. He rose into the air, and in a few minutes was perched on Bow's shoulder. "The doors are opening!" he cried.

Bow gave a signal, and a hundred armed men appeared from among the trees and began their advance on the mountain.

As the doors rumbled slowly open, then swung wide, Bow shouted, "CHARGE!" and led the way into the mountain. Shower after shower of arrows whistled ahead of the men as they advanced. The bright light of torches sparkled on swords and spears held at the ready.

From deep in the mountain there came the savage roar of the monster. Bow's men answered with their war-cry: "ETHERIA! ETHERIA!"

But even as their war-cry echoed inside the mountain, there was a blast of fire from a stun-cannon battery. Hordak had taken no chances. His monster warrior was protected by artillery.

From the edge of the forest Adora watched as Bow and his men made a fighting retreat from the mountain. "We need help," she said to herself. "I'll have to get my brother Prince Adam of Eternia... as his other self – HE-MAN!"

Prince Adam was sitting reading in his private apartment in the royal palace of Eternia when his sister's message came. Cringer lay sleeping in front of the fire.

"Wake up, Cringer!" cried Adam. "We have work to do!" Drawing the Sword of Power he called,

"BY THE POWER OF GRAYSKULL!"

In an instant he was He-Man, mightiest man in the universe, and Cringer had become the fearless Battle-Cat.

She-ra was waiting to greet He-Man on his arrival in Etheria. Quickly she explained about the monster and Bow's unsuccessful attack on the mountain. He-Man drew his sword, and Battle-Cat growled deep in his throat as he thought of the fight about to begin.

From a safe distance, Bow and his men watched as the monster came out of the mountain, moving slowly. Suddenly it roared with rage. In the light of the moon there was a flash of white as Swift Wind dived out of the night sky. At the same moment Battle-Cat charged with a snarl.

While She-ra circled just out of reach above the monster, He-Man aimed his sword and sent a blast

of energy zipping towards it. The shot hit the monster squarely... but passed through it without doing it any harm. He fired again and again. She-ra blasted at the creature with *her* energy weapon, but it did not even slow down!

Leaping from Battle-Cat, He-Man threw himself at the monster. But as he tried to come to grips with it, he found himself clutching at empty air!

Next moment He-Man felt himself seized by two powerful hands and hurled through the air. He landed with a thump. "I don't believe it," he cried as he pulled himself to his feet. "I couldn't get a grip on it... but it certainly got a grip on *me*!"

The monster had already disappeared into the night to spread further terror and destruction. Bow

and his men gathered around He-Man. "Let's get after it!" they cried.

"No," said She-ra. "This thing is no ordinary creature. It will not be beaten by ordinary means."

Kowl flew down. "Ahem, if I may be so bold... ...the monster is one of Shadow Weaver's creatures. It is not flesh and blood. It is a thing of dark magic and... *shadow*! I have a plan!"

Kowl explained. "The monster cannot withstand the power of light. That is why Hordak must keep it in the dark heart of the mountain. That is why he only lets it out at night, and why it must be safely inside again before daybreak."

"But," said Bow, "it walks the land in the light of the moon without harm. Our torches did it no harm either."

"There is only one light which can hurt the monster," said Kowl. "The light of the sun! Let the sun shine upon it and it is finished. Here is my plan."

In a few minutes everything was ready. She-ra and Bow led half the men in pursuit of the monster. He-Man went with the rest into the forest to carry out the second part of Kowl's plan. It would rid Etheria for ever of the monster from the Dark Pool.

Mounted on Swift Wind, She-ra flew through the night sky until she saw the black shape of the monster below. Swooping low, she circled it while it reached out to seize her.

Soon the men arrived, and formed a wide circle around the creature, just out of reach. They shouted at it. They threatened it with their weapons. Each time it lunged at them they drew back to a safe distance again.

All through the night they played this dangerous game with the evil creature. And all the time they

were luring it out of the forest. Soon the last of the trees were far behind. When the sky began to brighten in the east the monster was in the middle of open grassland. As the sun appeared over the horizon the monster shrieked with terror. But it was far from the shelter of the mountain or the thick forest.

In the light of the morning sun it began to dissolve. Soon there was nothing left of it but a patch of shadow in the grass. Then that too faded and disappeared.

The shadow had scarcely vanished when there was a swirl of darkness on the spot where the monster had melted in the sun. With a terrible laugh, Shadow Weaver stepped forward.

"You fools!" she cried. "You think you can win by destroying one of my creatures. I shall set free from the Dark Pool a whole army of monsters, each ten times more terrible than the one you have destroyed!"

With another laugh, she disappeared again.

"It's all up to He-Man and the rest of our men, now," said Bow.

In an open glade close to the Dark Pool, Shadow Weaver stood and listened. Instead of the deathly silence there were voices! She glided through the trees. The Dark Pool was no more!

The tangled trees which had kept out the sun were gone. They lay where they had been felled by the woodcutters' axes and the mighty strength of He-Man. The water sparkled as it caught the breeze and reflected the blue of the morning sky. The slime and poisonous moss shrivelled and died in the golden light.

Shadow Weaver knew that once again she had been beaten by the Power of Light.

He-Man mounted Battle-Cat, ready to return to Eternia.

As the people of Etheria crowded around to say goodbye, Bow said, "How can we ever thank you for what you have done?"

"Do not thank me," said He-Man. "I did very little. It was the wisdom of Kowl and the bravery of the people of Etheria which defeated Shadow Weaver and her monster."

She-ra stepped forward and said, "Goodbye, He-Man. We will never forget how you came to our aid."

"Goodbye!" cried He-Man, then he and Battle-Cat were gone.

The Twiggets came running up with all sorts of flowering plants, followed by Madame Razz. "We thought that we would plant these around the Dark Pool," they said.

"Not the Dark Pool," said She-ra. "From this day on it will be called the Golden Pool." And as she rode away through the Whispering Wood, she became Princess Adora once more.